Competitor Analysis:
WORKING PAPER

Competitor Analysis:
WORKING PAPER

Jacob Varghese

authorHOUSE®

AuthorHouse™
1663 Liberty Drive
Bloomington, IN 47403
www.authorhouse.com
Phone: 1-800-839-8640

© 2011 by Jacob Varghese. All rights reserved.

No part of this book may be reproduced, stored in a retrieval system, or transmitted by any means without the written permission of the author.

First published by AuthorHouse   11/21/2011

ISBN: 978-1-4678-7403-8 (sc)
ISBN: 978-1-4678-7402-1 (ebk)

Library of Congress Control Number: 2011960732

Printed in the United States of America

Any people depicted in stock imagery provided by Thinkstock are models, and such images are being used for illustrative purposes only. Certain stock imagery © Thinkstock.

This book is printed on acid-free paper.

Because of the dynamic nature of the Internet, any web addresses or links contained in this book may have changed since publication and may no longer be valid. The views expressed in this work are solely those of the author and do not necessarily reflect the views of the publisher, and the publisher hereby disclaims any responsibility for them.

List of Contents

1.1	Introduction	1
1.2	Environmental Scanning	3
1.2.1	Steps in connecting data to intelligence	4
1.2.2	The 80/20 rule-Primary Vs Secondary	4
1.2.3	Phase I Secondary research leads to Primary research	4
1.2.4	Phase II Primary Research	4
1.2.5	Comparison of Secondary & Primary Sources	5
1.3	The Need of Competitive Intelligence system	6
1.4	Identifiable steps in Competitive Intelligence gathering	6
1.4.1	Self assessment	6
1.4.2	Secondary sources	7
1.4.3	Types of secondary data	8
1.4.4	Types of secondary data	8
2	Competitor analysis	9
2.0.1	Theory of Analysis	9
2.0.2	Theory of search	9
2.0.3	Theory of choice	9
2.1	Competitor analysis frame work	9

2.2	Competitor's current strategy	10
2.2.0.1	Company History First Choice—SEC Filings	11
2.2.0.2	Trade news /special reports	11
2.2.1	Second choice—Industry Interviews	11
2.2.1.1	Stock trading statistics	12
2.2.1.2	Market studies	12
2.2.1.3	State corporate filings	12
2.2.1.4	Commercial databases	12
2.2.2	Third choice-Text books	12
2.2.2.1	Local business schools	13
2.2.3	Patent analysis—Data	13
2.2.3.1	Information	14
2.2.3.2	Intelligence	14
2.2.3.3	Identify the scope of the specific technology	15
2.2.3.4	Current Impact Index	15
2.2.4	SWOT analysis of competitiors	16
2.2.4.1	Strengths	16
2.2.4.2	Weakness	16
2.2.4.3	Opportunities	17

List of Contents

2.2.4.4	Threats	17
2.2.5	Competitor Positioning report	18
2.2.6	How do Companies Compete	18
2.2.6.1	First, Companies compete with products	18
2.2.6.2	Second companies compete in the financial area	19
2.2.6.3	Third, Companies compete in technology	19
2.2.6.4	Fourth,Companies compete with their organisations & people	19
2.2.6.5	Fifth, Companies compete by strategic alliances & other companies	19
2.2.6.6	Sixth, Companies compete in Manufacturing	19
2.2.6.7	Seventh, Companies compete in Marketing and advertising	19
2.2.6.8	Eighth, Companies compete with their reputation	19
2.2.7	Internet Intelligence	21
2.2.7.1	Databases	21
2.2.7.2	Databases with Data	21
2.3	Competitor'sFuture Objectives	21
2.3.1	Databases with stories	21
2.3.2	Decision Making Analysis	22

Assembling Management Profiles

2.3.3	First choice—Local Newspapers	23
2.3.3.1	Who's who Directories	23
2.3.3.2	D & B Credit reports	24
2.3.3.3	Annual report & Proxy	24
2.3.4	Second Choice Voter registry and assessor's office	24
2.3.4.1	Voter registry and assessor's office	25
2.3.5	Third choice Trade Journals	25
2.3.5.1	Trade associations	25
2.4.	Competitior's assumption	25

Interview techniques

2.4.1.0	Point 1 Explain who you are and why you are calling	26
2.4.1.1	Point 2 Have a name at hand	26
2.4.1.2	Point 3 When in doubt ; ask for public relations personnel	26
2.4.1.3	Point 4 Don't know it all;don't act tough	26
2.4.1.4	Point 5 Smile When you Dial	27
2.4.1.5	Point 6 Be humble,be naive	27
2.4.1.6	Point 7 To get a response, feed information	27

2.4.1.7	Point 8 Bracket Data	27
2.4.1.8	Point 9 Say you were referred	28
2.4.1.9	Point 10Exchange Information	28
2.4.2.	Sense of timing or How you make sure you reach the expert	28
2.4.2.1	Point 1 Don't call on Mondays	28
2.4.2.2	Point 2 Mornings are better than afternoons	28
2.4.2.3	Point 3 try to contact twice, and then calk back once more	29
2.4.2.4	Point 4 Don't overkill	29
2.4.2.5	Point 5 Set up a call back time	29
2.4.2.6	Point 6 tell the respondent how long the interview will be	29
2.4.3	Expert Interviews	30
2.4.4	Empirical Conversation	30
2.4.5	Expert: Regional Manager & Sales Manager and Interviewer	31
2.4.5.1	Question 1	31
2.4.5.2	Question 2	31
2.4.5.3	Question 3	32
2.4.5.4	Question 4	32

2.4.5.5	Question 5	33
2.4.5.6	Question 6	33
2.4.5.7	Question 7	33
2.4.5.8	End Conversation	34
2.4.6	Content Analysis	34
2.4.6.1	Data	34
2.4.7	Pricing Strategy	35

Data source for on how to prepare for trade show Intelligence

2.4.7.1	Target the key shows	35
2.4.7.2	Identify your internal experts ahead of time	36
2.4.7.3	Hold a pre—show meeting	36
2.4.7.4	Debrief during the show	36
2.4.7.5	Go to off-the floor networking meeting	36
2.4.7.6	Make communications easy	37
2.4.7.7	Hold a post-show analysis and meeting	37
2.4.8	Information	37
2.4.9	Trade Show Intelligence	38
2.5	Competitor's Resources and Capabilities	39
2.5.1	Capabilities	39

Financial analysis

2.5.2	List Objective	40
2.5.3	First Choice—SEC documents	40
2.5.3.1	Credit Report	40
2.5.3.2	Trade news article	40
2.5.4	Second Choice—Competitors-UCC filings	41
2.5.4.1	General corporate database	41
2.5.4.2	General Press	41
2.5.4.3	Town assessor's office	41
2.5.4.4	Real estate Agents	42
2.5.4.5	Courts	42
2.5.5	Third choice—Industry financial ratios	42
2.5.5.1	Interviews	42
2.5.5.2	Visual Sightings	42

Financial ratios

2.5.6	Debt Analysis—Company Debt Picture	43
2.5.6.1	Liquidity ratios	43
2.5.6.2	Data—Banks—BOS	43
2.5.6.3	Acid Test ratio	44
2.5.6.4	Data—Banks—BOS	44

List of Contents

2.5.7	Data—Financial leverage ratio	45
2.5.7.1	Information—debt—to—equity ratios	46
2.5.7.2	Intelligence	46
2.5.8	Data—Profitability Ratio	46
2.5.8.1	Information—Profitability ratios	46
2.5.8.2	Intelligence ROE	47
2.5.8.3	Calculating ROE for Bio technology Industries	47
2.5.9	Intelligence and assumptions in two perspectives	48
2.5.9.1	Banker perspective	48
2.5.9.2	Stock Holder Perspective	48
2.5.9.3	What is the current ROE ?	49
2.5.9.4	How deep should this start—up pockets be	49
2.5.9.5	Who manages the company?	49
2.5.9.6	Modifying the ratios through interviews	50
2.5.9.7	Example of steps in uncovering financial data using ratios	50
2.6	Competitor response Profile	50
2.6.1	Offensive moves	51
2.6.1.1	Satisfaction with current position	51

2.6.1.2	Probable moves	51
2.6.1.3	Strength & seriousness of moves	51
2.6.2	Defensive capability	51
2.6.2.1	Vulnerability	52
2.6.2.2	Provocation	52
2.6.2.3	Effectiveness of retaliation	52
2.7	Competitor Analysis and Industry Forecasting	53

Introduction

1.1 Given that competitor analysis is an essential component of corporate strategy, Porter(1980) argued that most firms do not conduct this type of analysis systematically enough. Rather, a lot of firms operate on what he calls "informal impressions, conjectures, and intuition gained through the tidbits of information about competitors every manager continually receives." As a result, traditional environmental scanning places many firms at risk of dangerous competitive blind spots due to lack of robust competitor analysis. To rectify this situation, Iam wirting this working paper to make easy for students to study and understand.

1.2 Environment Scanning[1] or competitive intelligence is a rigorous approach to collecting, analyzing and communicating information about competitors' activities, market changes that are occurring, changes related to the supply of raw materials, and other issues that could affect strategic directions. Such information is legally and ethically obtained from a wide range of sources using formalised techniques and can be factored into decision making.

Societal environment[2]

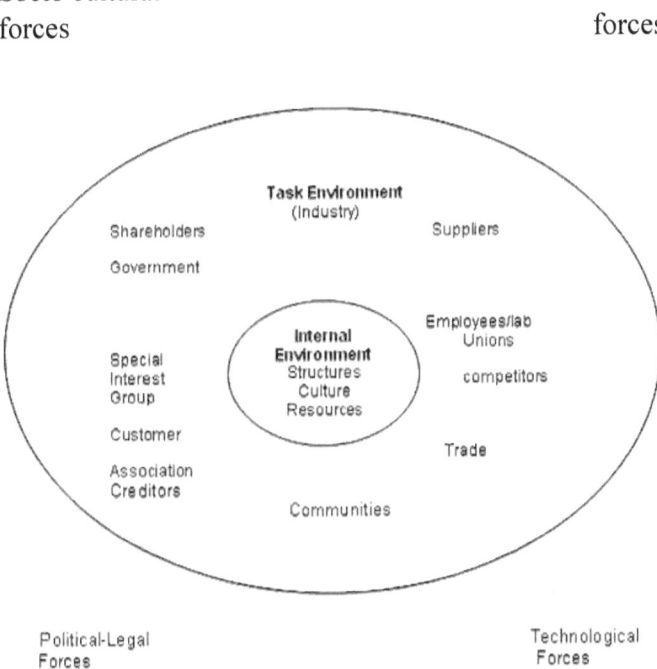

---

[1] Marylynn Placet and Christi m. Branch Pg 8
[2] www.environmentvariables.com

1.2.1 Steps in connecting data to intelligence[3]

Competitive Intelligence dwells on gathering data, analysing the gathered information and reproducing intelligence on the bases of the gathered information.

Data: Unconnected pieces of information
Information: Increased knowledge derived by understanding the relationships of data.
Intelligence: Organizing the information to fully appreciate the implications and impact on the organization.

1.2.2 The 80 / 20 Rule—Primary vs. Secondary[4]

Competitive intelligence follows a two phase process when it comes to collecting information:

Phase I : Secondary Research (80% volume/20%time)
Phase II : Primary Research (20% volume/ 80% time)

1.2.3 Phase I Secondary Research leads to Phase II primary research.
Secondary research consists of press releases, analyst reports, trade journals, regulatory filings, transcripts of speeches, and other published sources of information. The bulk of the information (let's say 80% of it) that we collect comes through secondary research. Once you shift through this information overload, we move to Phase II where the "golden nuggets" of competitive intelligence reside.

1.2.4 Phase II [4]Primary research is more hands-on and direct, interviewing sources of Published information,

---

[3] http://www.exinfm.com/training/course12-1/index.htm
[4] http://www.exinfm.com/training/course12-1/index.htm

meeting face-to-face with key decision makers and flushing out the critical unknowns not found in secondary research. It is here, primary Research, where we should spend most of the time (80%) on the pertinent information (20%) derived from secondary research. Therefore, we should recognize the 80/20 rule of competitive intelligence :Spend less of one's time gathering the information and spend more of one's time analyzing and refining it through primary research. This does not mean that secondary sources are less important or even less accurate that primary sources.

	Secondary Research	Primary Research
Volume of Data	80%	20
Time Spent	20%	80%

1.2.5 Comparison[5] of secondary and Primary sources

Secondary sources can sometimes be better sources of information than primary sources. One can get insightful opinions from analysts and journalists. These people may often see an entire industry and offer sides which one may not see (assumption).They may observe trends one has not noticed and have confidential sources within the industry. Secondary research tends to be easier than primary research since secondary sources of information are public knowledge.

Primary research is more difficult because you are on a detective hunt, trying to track down loose ends. Primary

---

[5] Page 55,Larry kahader

research is often done through a telephone interview, such as contacting suppliers, customers, business writers, and government agencies. Surveys are sometimes used where several sources are involved.

1.3 The Need for a Competitive Intelligence system[6]

Intelligence data on competitor's can come from many sources. Reports filed publicly, speeches by a competitor's management to security analysts, the business press, the sales force, a firm's customers or suppliers that are common to competitors. The elements of competitor Intelligence system can vary according to the particular firm's need, based in its industry.

1.4 Identifiable steps in Competitive Intelligence Gathering[7]

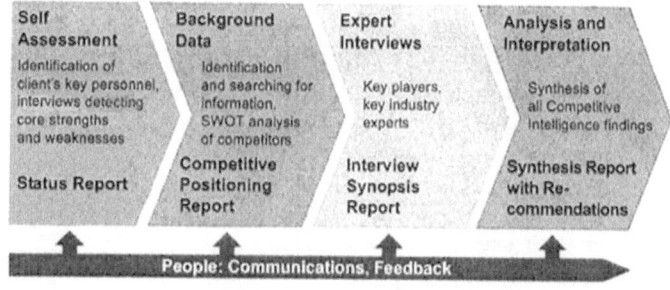

1.4.1. Self Assessment[8]:
Identification of client's key personnel, interviews detecting core strengths and weaknesses.

---

[6] Porter 1980, pg 71
[7] www.tns-infratest.com/pmwa
[8] http://www.exinfm.com/training/course12-1/index.htm

Status Report:

1) Financial ratios
2) Operating Cycle times
3) Work force statistics
4) Sources of revenue (Fees, contract, passive sources, etc)
5) Expenditure profile (operating, marketing, depreciation, etc)
6) Asset composition (current, fixed, leased, overseas, etc
7) Capital structure (debt level, interest rates, cost of capital, etc)
8) Overhead rates
9) Strategy, operating decisions, and tactical decisions
10) Organizational layout, functions, and business units
11) Processes (including taking a tour of your own facilities

1.4.2 Background Data from Secondary sources:

Gathering data from published and publicly available sources, including major competitors:

1) Press releases
2) Analyst reports
3) Trade journals
4) Regulatory filings
5) Transcripts of speech and other published sources of information
6) Financial reports
7) Academic Papers, Theses

1.4.3 Secondary sources[9]:
1) Private groups as foundation
2) Publishers
3) Trade association publications
4) Unions
5) Companies
6) Government census Department
7) Various registration offices (births, deaths, marriages, IT returns, employment offices, export declaration, automobile registration).
8) Taped and edited TV and radio interviews
9) Information sources from Newspapers, magazines, television, and radio

1.4.4 Types of Secondary Data

Hard	**Soft**
Facts	Rumours
Statistics	Opinions
Raw Data	Anecdotes
Financial Information	Op-ed pieces
News	Customer feed back

In short hard information is quantitative and soft information is qualitative[10]

---

[9] larry kahader pg 54 & 55
[10] Larry kahader, Pg 124

2.0 Competitor Analysis
Strategic Planning theory is divided into three parts:

2.0.1 Theory of analysis[11]: analysing the internal and external environment of the firm to determine what the current state is. The well-known SWOT analysis is the culmination of such strategic analysis;

2.0.2. Theory of search[12]: This includes the development of the picture of the firm's desired future and generating alternative ways of reaching the future.

Theory of choice: evaluating and choosing among the alternatives to find the ones consistent with the firm's mission and most likely to lead it to bridge the gap between its current state and desired future.

2.0.3. Theory of choice[13]: evaluating and choosing among the alternatives to find the ones consistent with the firm's mission and most likely to lead it to bridge the gap between its current state and desired future.

2.1. Competitor analysis frame work
There are four diagnostic components to a competitor analysis[14]. Future goals, current strategy, assumptions, and capabilities. Understanding these four components will allow an informed prediction of the competitor's response profile.

---

[11] Arnold Wentzel, Pg 3
[12] Arnold Wentzel, Pg 3
[13] Arnold Wentzel, Pg 3
[14] Porter,1980 Pg 48

Competitor's Current Strategy

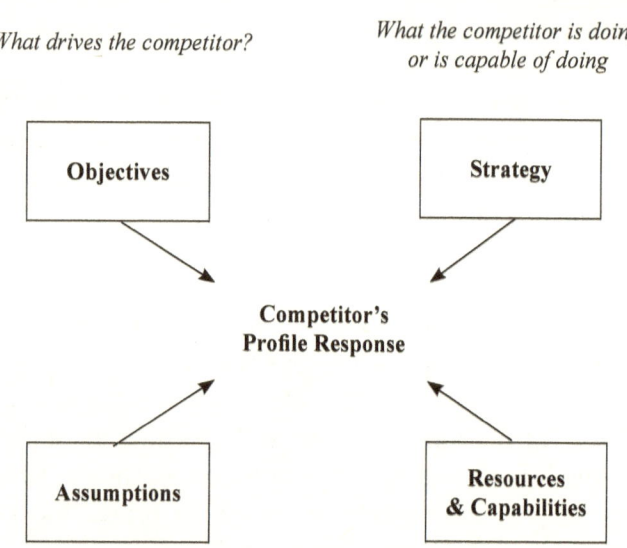

2.2 Competitor's current strategy[15]

There are two main sources of information about competitor's present strategy's what the competitor says and what it does. What a competitor says about is strategy?

However, this stated strategy often differs from what the competitor actually is doing. What the competitor is actually doing is evident in where its cash flow is directed, such as in the following tangible actions.

---

[15] http://www.netmba.com/strategy/competitor-analysis/

a) Hiring activity
b) R&D projects
c) Capital investments
d) Strategic partnerships
5) Mergers and acquisitions

Basic sources for Company history[16]

2.2.0.1 First choice—Data: SEC Filings
Information: The SEC's 10-K offer company history and management analysis sections, but only for publicly trading companies.
Intelligence: Discusses a new corporation and its brief history

2.2.0.2 Data: trade news/Special reports.
Information: Trade magazines feature at least one company per issue, profiling the company.
Intelligence: The articles are rich with company stories and activities. Select a most likely magazine and call up their editors or library. It will help you procure the recently published article on your target company.

2.2.1 Second Choice[17]—Data: Industry interviews
Information: Competitors, suppliers, and others
Intelligence: It helps you get a fair idea of the company's background.

---

[16] Leonard M. fuld 56
[17] Leonard M. fuld Pg 57

2.2.1.1-Data: Stock trading statistics
Information: e.g., Standard's and Poor's daily stock reports
Intelligence: It allows the researcher to track the progress of a company's stock, how it is traded, and whether there were any splits.

2.2.1.2-Data: Market studies
Information: Capsule reports describing a company may be contained within a larger market research report.
Intelligence: The company summaries are usually very general. The information is considerably dated. It is usually not worth your while to purchase an entire research study to obtain a one-or-two paragraph write-up of the company

2.2.1.3-Data: State corporate filings
Information: Most states require a company to file initial articles of incorporation and amendments

2.2.1.4-Data: Commercial databases
Information: One can find publicly traded companies described in Disclosure's database.
Intelligence: The articles discussed in the databases can lead you to the target company.

2.2.2 Third choice[18] **Data**: Text books
Information: It covers the history of a company
Intelligence: Finding the right book, with proper index is slim.

---

[18] Leonard M.Fuld Pg 57

2.2.2.1 Data: Local business schools
Information: University business schools conduct their own reviews of various companies. Most likely, a professor will select a company that is close to the school so that he or she can conduct interviews and on-site visits.
Intelligence: Try to locate a study on a local company by looking for the nearby business school.

2.2.3 Patent Analysis—Data

- Which companies are doing cutting-edge work; that the leaders are.
- Which individuals are doing cutting-edge work
- Which countries are on the forefront of a technology?
- .How long it takes companies to exploit a patent; how long it takes for research and development to turn into profits
- Which technologies are trending up or down; where R& D dollars are being spent among the industry leaders.
- Relationships(i.e.,jointventures)amongcompanies engaged in similar research or producing the same products, research relationships among company subsidiaries. There are two analytical approaches to patent search[19]

---

[19] Ashton & Sen 1988 Pg 42-46

2.2.3.1 Information:
The following information is contained in patent documents[20]

Claims: Description about the product or process. Claims also includes drawings and charts.

Inventor(s)/Author(s). This is the person or persons who actually invented the product and charts

Assignee. This is the person or company to whom the inventor assigned the patent. Usually an inventor working for a company will assign the patent to that company.

Licensee: The person or company to who has the right to produce the invention under agreement with the patent holder.

Citations. Patents are issued only for new or novel inventions; no one has to reinvent the wheel. All patents must cite other patents from which the current work has used facets of or improved upon[21].

2.2.3.2 Intelligence;
About 70% to 80% of all patents are never cited[22] by another inventor in his patent. Therefore when one particular patent is cited continually[23], it shows that the assignee owns some leading edge technology. There for if a company is heavily citing patents it indicates that it is building large body of knowledge in that area and will exploit that technology to its fullest. These companies may be employing a Pioneer strategy

---

[20] Larry kahader Pg 113
[21] Campbell 1983 Pg 62-67;Karki,1997 Pg 269-272
[22] Karki, 1997 Pg 269-272
[23] Craig Fleisher & barbara bensoussan Pg 349

E.g.: Hitachi in next page

2.2.3.3. Identify the scope of the specific technology. Companies that cite other companies' patents are engaging in a imitator strategy, relying on the work of others to boost their own efforts. In the other way, a company whose patents are cited more often than it may be losing its technology lead to its competitors.

Technological strength = (number of patents) * CII

2.2.3.4 Current Impact Index (CII). This index essentially translates the absolute number of highly cited patents into a relative index to facilitate comparison across patents

CII= Average citations per firm patent each year / Average number of citations of all patents in the database per year

Citations for Hitachi

24

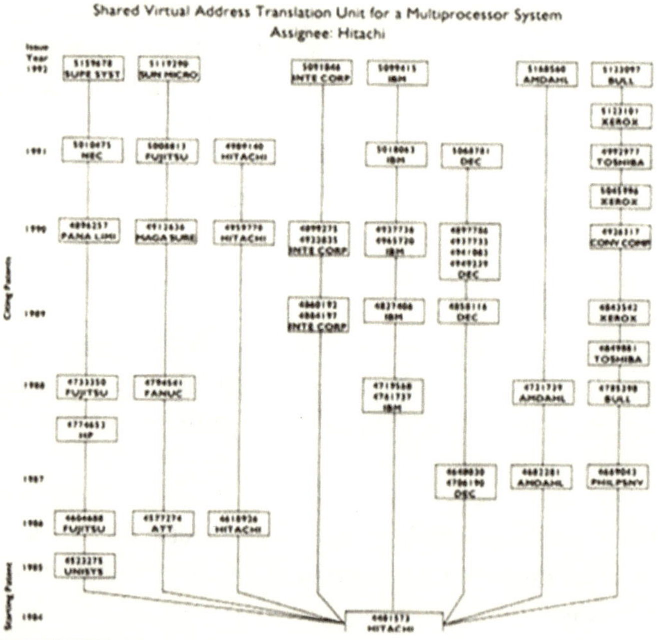
Shared Virtual Address Translation Unit for a Multiprocessor System
Assignee: Hitachi

2.2.4 SWOT analysis of competitors[25]

2.2.4.1 Strength includes the competitor's most powerful attributes, including the patents it holds, its technology, market share, depth of management, financial position, customer loyalty, quality of product, and so forth.

2.2.4.2 Weakness are opposite of strengths and include the competitor's liabilities such as weighty debt, unskilled

---

24 larry kahader Pg 114

25 Larry Kahader Pg 99

workers, labour strife, poor-quality products, poor image, and Outmoded equipment processes

2.2.4.3 Opportunities are chances to prosper from a changing marketplace, industry situation, or other environmental condition. Opportunities include things like pending government regulation that would benefit the company, changing demographics that boost the potential customer base, a competitor's patent that is expiring, or a drastic drop in the cost of raw materials.

2.2.4.4 Threats are the opposite of opportunities in that they are external conditions that can harm a company. These include raw materials shortages, costly government regulations, new competitors, or, for companies that rely on borrowing money, interest rates that are heading higher.

Strengths and Weaknesses are internal Characteristics and Opportunities and threats are external Characteristics.

SWOT gives way of analyzing a competitor by filling in a matrix of the company's characteristics. SWOT is more of a qualitative analysis as opposed to a financial analysis

SWOT MATRIX of Company A [26]

Internal Factors → External Factors ↴	Strengths (S) 1. Best technology 2. Skilled workforce	Weaknesses (W) 1. No management depth 2. Spotty distribution
Opportunities (O) 1. Demographics favor product consumption 2. Failing of other competitor, B	SO Implications 1-1 Keep technology current 2-2 Might hire skilled workers from B	WO Implications 2-1 Must satisfy growing market segment to remain competitive
Threats (T) 1. Possible regulation 2. Growing of competitor C	ST Implications 1-1 Might have to share technology to avoid regulation 2-2 Keep current workforce satisfied	WT Implications 1-1 Management may not be able to thwart regulation 2-2 C may take market share away

2.2.5 Competitor Positioning Report:[27]
SWOT gives way of analyzing a competitor by filling in a matrix of the company's characteristics. SWOT is more of a qualitative analysis as opposed to a financial analysis.

2.2.6 How Do Companies Compete?[28]
Key: What makes a company competitive and in what areas do you and your competitor go head-to-head?

2.2.6.1 First, companies compete with products. They strive for quality, market share, and performance of their product, low returns, and customer satisfaction with the product.

---

[26] Larry kahader Pg 102
[27] Larry Kahader Pg 98
[28] Leonard M.fuld Pg 100

2.2.6.2 Second, companies compete in the financial area. Companies want high returns on return on investment, high share price, low costs, and access to capital when necessary.

2.2.6.3 Third, companies compete in technology. They want to bring products to market quickly. They want to exploit their patents and prevent others from using them. They want to get high returns on research and development dollars.

2.2.6.4 Fourth, companies compete with their organizations and their people. They want depth in management, a corporate culture that breeds success, and a highly trained, intelligent workforce.

2.2.6.5 Fifth, companies compete by strategic alliances with other companies. To build strength they acquire the skills of other companies by merger or joint ventures. Successful companies have strong alliances with suppliers, distributors, and manufacturers.

2.2.6.6 Sixth, companies compete in manufacturing. Some of this can over lap with product competition, but mainly we're talking about plant capacity, special processes and machinery, motivated and skilled labour force, and, of course, quality.

2.2.6.7 Seventh, companies compete with marketing and advertising. Areas such as service and strong promotion are key factors here. **2.2.6.8 Eighth, companies compete with their reputation**. How they are perceived by the media, customers, suppliers, financial institutions, and government agencies are important factors in a firm's competitive edge

In this typical matrix with an example of a company A's SWOT. As you assess your competitors look in the above eight areas to decide which factors are crucial to their success. Also notice in the matrix that it not only has implications but possible scenarios as well. There won't be a one-to-one-correlation on every cross factor nor will only one implication spring from each factoring of SWO and T. In this example are many more possible scenarios.

How do Companies Compete[29]

Products
- quality
- market share
- performance
- low returns

Financials
- low debt
- high share price
- access to capital

Technology
- cutting-edge
- fast cycle times
- high patent exploitation

Organization
- skilled/trained workers
- motivated workforce
- depth in management

Alliances
- strong joint ventures
- strong relationships with other companies, suppliers, distributors, and customers

Manufacturing
- special processes
- necessary capacity
- up-to-date machinery

Marketing/Advertising
- strong promotions
- healthy budget

Reputation/Image
- positive perception
- name recognition
- trademark recognition

---

[29] Larry Kahader, Pg 102

2.2.7. Internet Intelligence[30]

2.2.7.1 Databases: databases are excellent tools for casting a wide net to begin your information search. You can either hook up directly to the database itself or have a company do the search for you based on key words. There are two categories of divide for databases. Those with stories and those with data.

2.2.7.2 Data base with Data[31]: Those Databases with data carry patents, financial information, advertising, stock exchange information, statistics, and sales-unfiltered, raw data. These are primary sources but a few secondary sources as well

2.3. Competitor's Future Objectives
Knowledge of a competitor's objectives facilitates a better prediction of a competitor's reaction to different competitive moves. Competitor objectives may be financial or other types. Market share, growth rate, technology leadership etc.

2.3.1 Databases with stories contain articles from newspapers, magazines; transcriptions of TV and radio shows, newsletters, press releases, government reports. These are usually "secondary sources." These are usually secondary sources but a few primary too. Those databases with data carry patents, financial information, advertising, stock exchange information, statistics, sales—unfiltered

---

[30] Larry kahader, Pg 70
[31] Larry kahader, Pg 69

raw data. These are mainly primary sources but a few secondary sources as well

Databases with stories[32]

INVESTEXT	Reports from Wall Street analysts
ABI/INFORM	Abstracts and full text of business journals
DOW JONES NEWS RETRIEVAL	Full text of *Wall Street Journal* and other periodicals
DATATIMES	Full text of hundreds of newspapers
NEWSNET	Full text of more than 300 newsletters

Databases with Data

DUN'S MARKET IDENTIFIERS	More than 6 million records about companies
DRI INTERNATIONAL AUTO	Automobile production figures in many countries
FINANCIAL TIMES CURRENCY AND SHARE INDEX	Data on international exchange rates
TELERATE	Securities prices

2.3.2 Decision making analysis :

Executives vary widely in how much they scan as well as their use of different sources of learning about external events or trends[33] An executive's orientation consists of

---

[32] Larry kahader Pg 114

[33] Keflas & Schoderbeck,1973 Pg 63-74; Hambrick 1982 Pg 159-172

an interwoven set of psychological characteristics and observable experiences[34]:

- Psychological properties such as values, cognitive models, and other personality traits.
- Observational experiences are those dimensions of the person's experiences: such as functional background, company tenure, and formal education

Assembling Management profiles[35]

2.3.3 First choice: **Data**: Local Newspapers
Information: Very often, a national press release on a executive's promotion will only be carried in his or her hometown newspaper or in the newspaper where the plant or office is located.
Intelligence: Local newspapers may have also done a feature story on the executive, especially if the executive or the company he or she works for contributes to the economic health of the community.

2.3.3.1-Data: Who's Who directories
Information: There are many varieties of biographical directories. Some, like Marquis' Who's Who in Finance and Industry, cover all industries and the major executives in each. Other directories are geared toward one industry, such as Who's who in Electronics.
Intelligence: A Who 's Who will list only 5 percent or fewer of those you might consider important executives,

---

[34] Finkelstein & hambrick,1996 Pg 41
[35] Leonard M. fuld Pg 55

It is important to notice that one should not get surprised if one does not find one's candidate companies.

2.3.3.2 Data: D & B Credit Reports.
Information: D & B reports, and others like them, are designed to analyze a Company, not its officers, although frequently the reports include some form of Biographical sketch.

Intelligence: The Reports are useful to start assembling a biography of a executive. e.g., It may tell you where an executive attended school and where he or she lives. These may lead to follow through on: contact X and the local newspaper Y or a Rotary club Z.

2.3.3.3 Data: Annual report & proxy
Information: Annual reports sometimes contain brief rundowns on the senior executives. Proxies, on the other hand, list the company's officers in some detail.

Intelligence: The sources of information apply only to publicly held companies

2.3.4 Second choice-Data: Voter registry and assessor's offices
Information: A local town hall will record the number of occupants in a house and who owns the house, as well as the homeowner's age and the number of members in his or her family.

Intelligence: The above data can derive census in the recorded area.

2.3.4.1 Data: Colleague interviews
Information: Insights on the behaviour of a colleague
Intelligence: It can help to amplify the character of a colleague.

2.3.5. Third choice
Data: Trade journals
Information: Trade magazines will often cover many of the industry's key promotions. Occasionally, they will write up a complete profile on one of its professionals who achieved industry greatness.
Intelligence: These articles reveal much about an executive's management style and financial wizardry.

2.3.5.1-Data: Trade Associations.
Information: Associations are very protective of their membership—and rightfully so. They will be happy to talk about the good things of an individual
Intelligence: Smaller trade associations are far more helpful and knowledgeable than are larger ones in regard to revelations of an individual. They know their members, who may number only in the hundreds, whereas an association with thousands of members is not likely to recall a particular name or face.

2.4. Competitor's Assumptions
The assumptions that a competitor's managers hold about their firm and their industry help to define the moves that they will consider.

A competitor's assumptions may be based on a number of factors.

a) Beliefs about its competitive position
b) Past experience with a product
c) Regional factors
d) industry trends

Interview techniques[36]: Knowing when and how to ask the right questions takes a combination of instinct and experience.

2.4.1-Point 1: **Explain who you are and why you are calling**: By doing so, you become a person, accountable to some corporation or organisation. You establish creditability and put the contact on ease.

2.4.1.1-Point 2: **Have a name at hand**: As for a specific person. By knowing the names and titles of knowledgeable sources, you eliminate fishing for experts and avoid run-arounds.

2.4.1.2-Point 3: **when in doubt; ask for public relations or personnel**: PR people generally know who's who and what's what in a company. They can either put you in touch with the experts in their firm or direct you to outside sources. They can also dig up organisational data or industry statistics in a hurry.

2.4.1.3-Point 4: Don't know it all; don't act tough. No one who feels threatened is going to offer information. Likewise, no one will talk freely if you appear to already have all the information you need, or can easily get it elsewhere.

---

[36] Leonard M.fuld Pg 69

2.4.1.4-Point 5: Smile when you dial: If you smile and dial, your voice carries a message to the person on the other end. Human nature being what it is, people are always more receptive to exuberance than they are to ennui.

2.4.1.5-Point 6: **Be humble, be naive**: By claiming to know little or nothing about the subject-but desperately wanting to learn you will probably get a respondent to offer more information. Or, the person may feel sorry for you and refer you to another source. This technique also allows the researcher to ask questions until the information is clearly understood. In research, the only dumb question is the one that isn't asked

2.4.1.6-Point 7: **To get a response, feed information**: remember, you are calling people out of the blue. To help orient their thought and adjust them to your thinking, tell them some of what you have found out to date and what you still need. Tell them about some of the industry gossip you have heard. Also, mention the gaps that your research still has.

2.4.1.7-Point 8: bracket data. Many professionals refuse to give or feel hesitant in offering numbers or statistics off the top of their heads. They would rather refer to a textbook-which, of course is never handy when you are calling. So help the respondent by giving them range of numbers to work with.

E.g.," Do you think the sales are between $ 10 million and $15 million, or are we talking more in the range of $ 50 million to $75million?

2.4.1.8-Point 9: <u>**Say you were referred**</u>: referrals are door openers. Whenever you call some one based on a referral, make sure that your first sentence includes the name of the person who referred you.

2.4.1.9-Point 10: <u>**Exchange information**</u>—the maximum "You get nothing for nothing" holds very true when it comes to research. One will encounter a lot of resistance if one is pestering someone who will gain nothing from your questions. No one likes to feel milked. Except U.S government analysts for everyone else, however, swap information or offer to send them a small portion of the summary of the results (without sacrificing confidentiality or disclosing too much of the report).This is an especially effective technique when soliciting information from service professionals (marketing consultants, management consultants) who make their living dispensing advice. They are not likely to give you any information unless you can offer something in return.

2.4.2. Sense of timing or How to make sure you reach your expert[37]

2.4.2.1 Point 1: <u>Don't call on Mondays</u>. Mondays are the best time to reach experts and the worst time for getting them to talk to you. Probably because the experts may have left a number of pressing needs hanging from the Friday departure

2.4.2.2 Point 2: <u>Mornings are better than afternoons</u>. by Tuesday, a person is in the work week of mind. So the early

---

[37] Leonard m. fuld Pg 70

part of the workday is often the best time to reach executives. They have the fewest intrusions early in the day.

2.4.2.3 Point 3: <u>**Try to contact twice, and then call back once more:**</u> Three times should be enough. Your time is precious, too. If you do not find a potential respondent cooperative, then move on to the next one. Remember, there is always more than one expert.

2.4.2.4 Point 4: <u>Don't over kill</u>: although many people admire persistence, few welcome pests. Do not make oneself a nuisance. People may refuse you because they just do not have the time to give that week. If the interviewer creates a ill will at this first encounter, one may be closing the doors to any future contact or additional surveys one may have to conduct.

2.4.2.5 Point 5: <u>Set up a call back time</u>: If you set up a time to call back, the respondent will expect to hear from you and at least has to have some kind of answer to one's questions. Generally, a respondent appreciates that you respect his or her time enough to schedule the interview.

2.4.2.6 Point 6: <u>**Tell the respondent how long the interview will be**</u>. Never say the interview will take a few minutes. "Anyone who has ever received a consumer telephone survey call realises that the "few minutes" stated by the interviewer can often run into half an hour or more. Meanwhile, your supper has gone cold and your anger has heated up. Keep one's surveys relatively short, and always state a accurate time.

2.4.3. Expert Interviews:

The following disguised interview gives insights into the methods and techniques and ways to improve in expert interviews.

Lesson 1, Orient Your listener: You need to orient the person you interview.
Lesson 2, Limit the Scope of Your questions. Most experts will know only a few bits and pieces of information and not the entire answer. Do not keep pummelling the expert with questions in hopes of learning the entire answerably doing so, one will frustrate a possibly valuable contact. Instead, ask questions that are limited in scope and you will likely be rewarded with better than expected result.

2.4.4. Empirical conversation In this project, the analyst must identify and assess potential generic pharmaceutical competitors who are poised to launch a new class of drugs-anti-migraine medicines, in this fictionalised case. This is the big picture the analyst needs to understand. However, in the interview, the analyst lays out a far narrower set of objectives for himself
Needs to discover: The analyst needs to locate potential suppliers of a bulk chemical supplier.
Opportunities: If he can identify the bulk supplier, he has a good chance of discovering who the U.S and European generic marketers will be.

Competitor's Assumptions

2.4.5. Expert: Regional marketing and sales manager-interviewer[38]: Analyst.

2.4.5.1 Q 1 Interviewer: Hello, my name is Tom Moore and I am trying to understand the general direction the anti-migraine market is heading. Can you help me?
Comments: General opening asking for help, rather than sounding pompous and all-knowing is what you need to start.

Expert: No, I'm no pharmaceutical guru. My job is just to sell the bulk chemicals to the Marks of the world.
Comments: The expert is not who the analyst thought he might be. These surprises will often start a problem, and will end an interview prematurely. Don't let it. Persist and see if there is another opportunity to explore. After all, the expert did not say "no", he only said he did not feel confident enough to answer this question.

2.4.5.2 Q 2 Interviewer: I see, let me reword my question, if I can. If I can better understand the movement of the raw chemical used in this type of medication, then I can better assess the market's growth and players in this relatively new market. Does this help?
Comments: Note the analyst's response. He calmly restated his request, adjusting it to fit the knowledge base of the person he has in front of him.
Expert: Not really. You want me to divulge my clients 'marketing strategies. I'm sorry but even if I knew, I couldn't tell you. Sorry, but . . .

---

[38] Leonard M.fuld Pg 74

Competitor's Assumptions

Comment: Another potential barrier, perhaps the most difficult to overcome-confidentiality. What would you do here?

2.4.5.3 Q 3 Interviewer: No. I don't want you to reveal a confidence. Rather, if you could just tell me the general movement in this market, that would be helpful. You don't have to name names. Okay?

Comment: This is the most straightforward response the analyst could offer. The "Okay" at the end definitely gives the expert the option to stop the interview right here. It is a risk worth taking. Your goal is to get the bits and pieces of information you need, but not at all costs. Think of the practical side. You may have to speak to this person again near the end of the study. You want someone who will trust you, not someone who will hang up the phone.

Expert: Okay. What I can tell you is public knowledge and was widely spoken about at the last conference, held in Paris.

2.4.5.4 Q 4 Interviewer: I'd appreciate hearing more about this conference, or whatever you feel comfortable discussing.

Comment: Once again, the interviewer has chosen to emphasize the unthreatening aspect of the interview.

Expert: Poinsyntex, in San Celoni, Spain, is going back into the bulk oxyrib business. Poinsyntex had told Drug co AG in Germany that it plans to have product available by fourth quarter this year. One Poinsyntex's big markets will be the U.S., although it's not clear to whom it will sell the oxyrib.

Comment: Much of this conversation may not contain a great deal of new or valuable information. Yet it can lead the interviewer to other potentially valuable opportunities.

2.4.5.5 Q 5 Interviewer: Can you guess who the international buyers for oxyrib might be?
Comment: Notice that the interviewer asked the expert to guess who the buyers is, a piece of information the expert knows well since he deals in this market every day. At the same time, the expert is giving away little information that would in any way compromise a client.
Expert: My guess is Nippon PHARMA OF Japan; TJK also of Japan, Markkum in the U.S and Rikard Veber in the Netherlands. That is all I know. Sorry if my information is limited.

2.4.5.6 Q 6 Interviewer: No problem. You gave me some insight. By the way do you have names of people. I can speak to at Markkum and Veber?
Comment. Why stop here? If the expert knows the companies in question, he also must know people in those companies. So . . .
Expert: In Fact, yes. At Markkum, you want to call Peter Steen and at Veber, Johan Maas.

2.4.5.7 Q.7 Interviewer: thank you, once again. By the way, I came across a great investor's report on this market. Would you like a copy for your files?
Comment: In the process of conducting the research, the interviewer surely came across information he could give away without exposing his client or his client's purpose. This investment report might be in public domain, but

could be considered extremely valuable to the expert who did not know it existed. Now, the information swap that took place in this interview is more even-handed. Both parties the expert and the interviewer have benefited.
Expert: Sure that would be great.

2.4.5.8 Q.8 End conversation: I'll be happy to send it to you. Thanks again

2.4.6 Content Analysis[39]:

Identifying Intentions with Content Analysis: Content analysis and related techniques that try to identify underlying meanings from the words used by a competitor's executives or managers can help to clarify a competitor's intentions. Words are a mirror of the corporate Personality. If the text is appropriately selected, an informed analysis can "decode" the words and provide insights into corporate directions and priorities. The effectiveness of content analysis is sensitive to two factors.

- The source of the text, and
- The frame work for identifying themes.

2.4.6.1 Data: Content analysis of a top executive's speeches (or other documents fro public consumption) are more suspect if a speech writer is involved. It is better if the document is closer to unguarded speech.

---

[39] Leonard m.Fuld Pg 290

Information: Content analysis should start with the identification of the framework that includes the possible themes that are expected to appear.

2.4.7 Pricing strategy :
Intelligence Shopping at trade shows: Bag your competitor's strategy, instead of a few glossy brochures.

Trade show information exchanges[40]
The trade Show Bureau surveyed trade show attendees to ask them what actions they took at the last trade show they attended. This was their response

- 95% asked for literature to be sent.
- 95% saw and talked with current suppliers.
- 94% Compared similar products
- 77% Found at least one new supplier.
- 76% asked for a price quotation.
- 51% Requested a sales representative be sent to my company.
- 26% signed a purchase order

Data Source on how to prepare for the Trade show Intelligence[41]

2.4.7.1 Target the key shows:
Your strategic planning, market research group, or whoever is responsible for the competitive assessments, needs to identify the critical shows throughout the world.

---

[40] The power of trade shows: fact sheet # 3, Trade show bureau, Copyright 1992
[41] Leonard M. fuld Pg 326

2.4.7.2 Identify your internal experts ahead of time:
You may want to assemble your most experienced and technically knowledgeable people at the trade show. The way to do this is through an intelligence audit of the experts in your company. The expertise you should look for can range from competitor specific knowledge to understanding a particular chemical process. There is so much information flying around a trade show that only a multifunctional team can hope to capture it successful.

2.4.7.3 Hold a pre-show meeting:
A few days before the show, the team leader needs to assign trade show or conference attendees specific objectives. Hand out a checklist of what they need to look for. Include in the list key competitors and expected product or service announcements, and a map of the show floor with key booths marked.

2.4.7.4 Debrief during the show:
Constantly test your questions and hunches against trade show reality by bringing your team back to a specific booth or hotel room near the show floor where everyone can compare notes. These sessions also helped us disprove some potentially resource-draining rumours.

2.4.7.5 Go to off-the-floor networking meetings:
Some of the most vital conference or trade show information will come from informal, pick up meetings that may occur after the speaker has ended a talk. It is at these meetings that you will bump into the CEO or VP of Marketing for a large corporation. Often participants in such meetings will take the opportunity to ask some very

frank and pointed questions, the answers to which you do not want to miss.

2.4.7.6 Make communications easy: Too often all that a company has to show for its attendance is trade show literature, some formal memos, and expense reports. In order to act upon the significant pieces of news and intelligence your team develops from one of these shows, make sure team members are allowed to express themselves easily and freely. Arm your staff with cell phones, especially at the larger shows where you need to spread your team out geographically. You need them to stay in touch regularly.

2.4.7.7 Hold a post—show analysis and meeting[42]: Pull your team together at your offices once the show has ended. Find various public forums to report your conclusions. Identify major sales or staff meetings and ask the meeting chairperson to place you on his or her agenda.

2.4.8 Information: Each member of your vertical buying or intelligence team should receive an information packet describing current industry news, as well as thumbnail sketches of key companies, whether they be competitors, customers, or suppliers. One can make this a fairly simple job by using widely available library sources.

- Copies of competitors' advertisements
- Online news reports of your competitors that your librarian can supply by searching such database systems as Dow Jones, Nexis, or Dialog

---

[42] Leonard M.fuld Pg 327

- Pre-show planner and directory[43].
- Marked up map of the trade show floor, identifying each of the targeted booths your team will approach.
- Telephone numbers of key "information" staff back at your office for team Members to call if they have questions.

2.4.9 Trade Show Intelligence[44] a) Size and location, b) Number of people manning booth, c)Level of seniority among exhibitors, d)Amount of off-the-floor networking, e)Level of activity at hospitality suite. f) Back wall advertising slogans. g)New product displays, h)Types of literature given out, i)Themes or slogans used, j)Price sheets and stated terms, k)Attendee interest level.

Show Seminars
a) Topics and themes, b) Level of attendance, c) Identify which meetings target companies attend, d) Note questions asked and who asks them.

Product Demonstrations
a) Note questions asked, b) Product features, c)Availability and release date d) Bundling and pricing options, e) Level and sophistication of demonstrator.

Target Company's Technology
a) Identify technology changes, b) Note bundling of technology into product or service, c) Target company's

---

[43] Leonard M.fuld pg 327
[44] Leonard M.Fuld Pg 329

emphasis (or lack) on technology, d) Leading edge or old technology, e) System efficiency

2.5. Competitor's Resources and capabilities

Knowledge of the competitor's assumptions, objectives, and current strategy is useful in understanding how the competitor might want to respond to a competitive attack. However, its resources and capabilities determine its ability to respond effectively.

Resources are the firm specific assets useful for creating a cost or differentiation advantage and that few competitors acquire easily.

> Patents and trade marks
> Proprietary know-how
> Installed customer base
> Reputation of the firm
> Brand equity

2.5.1 Capabilities refers to the firm's ability to utilize its resources effectively. Such capabilities are embedded in the routines of the organization and are not easily documented as procedures and thus are difficult for competitors to replicate. A competitor's capabilities can be analyzed according to its strengths and weaknesses in various functional areas (SWOT Analysis). The competitor's strengths define its capabilities. The analysis can be taken further to evaluate the competitor's ability to increase its capabilities in certain areas. A financial analysis can be performed to reveal its sustainable growth rate.

Financial Analysis [45]

2.5.2. List objective: To help assemble a financial statement includes both those sources that directly contain company financials and those that can supply a portion of a financial statement (e.g., labour costs, plant assets) where no complete statement exists in the public domain.

2.5.3 First choice—Data: SEC documents—Annual report (secondary):
Information: 10-K annual report
Intelligence: Most public and some private corporations publish their own version of SEC's required 10-K annual report. It is designed to impress current and prospective stockholders. Yet, these annuals frequently contain the same income statement and balance sheet information as one would find in the 10-K.

2.5.3.1-Data: Credit report
Information: while short on financials, can sometimes pull together all the publicly filed financial information. Occasionally, a credit report will also reveal an income Statement for a privately held corporation.
Intelligence: These sales figures are, many times, estimates or unverified information given by the company itself

2.5.3.2-Data: Trade news article
Information: It discusses some financial information, plant size, number of employees, or sales

---

[45] Leonard M.fuld Pg 53

Intelligence: These articles look authoritative, but they are occasionally written by the company's public relations agency with only minor editing on the part of the magazine.

2.5.4 Second choice[46]-

Competitors: One can find that competitors are not only knowledgeable about their competition, but may also give one a good deal of information as part of a information swap.

Data: UCC filings
Information: It helps in disclosing useful information on a new plant asset on which one may target to take out a loan.

2.5.4.1-Data: General corporate Database.
Information: It offers addresses and some financial data on millions of companies privately held and publicly traded.

2.5.4.2 Data: General press
Information: It contains some financial details. It contains at least some information on sales and growth rate.

2.5.4.3-Data: Town Assessor's Office
Information: It supplies you with tax, ownership, and zoning information that the company may have filed.
Intelligence: The filings put together are often skimpy, but may still contain more data than are found in the state filing.

---

[46] Leonard M.fuld Pg 53

2.5.4.4-Data: Real Estate Agents
Information. A Real estate agent can give you information on the square footage costs of the company's plant and, perhaps, specifications on the plant and equipment.

2.5.4.5-Data: Courts
Information: Court filings may reveal details on a company's indebtedness or problems involving trademark infringement, Bankruptcy.

2.5.5 Third Choice[47]
Data: Industry financial ratios.
Information: If one has a few details on a few data items, such as sales and Current assets, one can construct a complex Income statement or balance Sheet using industry financial ratios.

2.5.5.1.—Data: Interviews
Information: Although not a scientific approach, interviews can occasionally reveal good guesstimates of a company's sales and assets.

2.5.5.2—Data: Visual sightings
Information: Counting the number of parking spaces and applying a rough Formula for number of riders per car will give you a approximately employment figure for a plant or office.

Financial ratios

---

[47] Leonard m.fuld Pg54

2.5.6 Debt analysis—Company debt picture: In the following financial ratios can be classified according to the information they provide. The following types of ratios frequently are used:

- Liquidity ratios
- Asset turnover ratio

2.5.6.1 Liquidity ratio[48] liquidity ratios provide information about a firm's ability to meet its short term financial obligations. They are of particular interest to those extending short-term credit to the firm. Two frequently-used liquidity ratios are the current ratio (or working capital ratio) and the quick ratio.

2.5.6.2 Data: Banks—BOS
Financial Statements and Operating Ratios for the Mortgage banking Industry

(Mortgage bankers Association of America, Economics and Education Department)

Or

Financial Companies-Analysis of year end Composite ratios of Instalment Sales Finance and Small Loan Companies (Journal of Commercial bank Lending, Robert Morris Associates)

Information: The current ratio is the result of current assets divided by current liabilities. Bankers and analysts

---

[48] Leonard m.fuld Pg 301

use the ratio to understand a company' ability to pay short term obligations-its liquidity.

Intelligence: A company is generally judged "liquid "if its current ratio is 2:1

Current ratio= Current asset/Current liabilities= eg $250,000/$125000=2.0

This 2:1 ratio is a fairly conservative number and may not reflect the particular

Industry one is examining, where the ratio may be closer to 1.5:1.Just using the 2:1 relationship, a banker would say that this company is a safe bet. What the banker is saying is that 50% of the current assets can be converted into cash reasonably fast.

2.5.6.3 Acid test ratio [49]

The current ratio becomes the acid-test ratio by eliminating any non cash assets, such as inventory.

2.5.6.4 Data:Banks-BOS

Information: The acid test assumes that, because inventory is not cash and could take weeks or months to be converted into cash, it is truly a liquid asset

Acid-test ratio= Cash Accounts + receivable/Total current liabilities= e.g.,125000/$125000=1.0

Intelligence the typical ratio is 1: 1.Anything below 1.0 may be considered financially precarious

---

[49] Leonard m.fuld Pg 301

Advice: You can draw several inferences from the quick ratio. For example.

A high quick ratio could indicate a very conservative, risk adverse competitor that is unwilling to leverage cash resources. On the other hand, a high quick ratio could signal that the competitor is poised to mount a competitive challenge—perhaps one that is already rumoured in the industry. To draw any final conclusions, you need to combine experts' comments with the quick ratios you have compiled. Gather other evidence of activity or inactivity before allowing the ratios themselves to lead you to a decision.

Intelligence: A company is generally judged "liquid "if its current ratio is 2:1

Current ratio= Current asset/Current liabilities= eg $250,000/$125000=2.0

This 2:1 ratio is a fairly conservative number and may not reflect the particular

Industry one is examining, where the ratio may be closer to 1.5:1.Just using the 2:1 relationship, a banker would say that this company is a safe bet. What the banker is saying is that 50% of the current assets can be converted into cash reasonably fast.

2.5.7 Data—Financial leverage ratio—: Stock holders' equity for annual reports, regulatory filings (such as Securities and Exchange Commission filings), credit reports, and some state or provincial government filings.

2.5.7.1 Information: **Debt-to-equity ratio**: This ratio compares total liabilities to stock holders' equity. In effect, it measures ineptness and solvency.

Debt/equity ratio[50]= Total liabilities/Total stockholders' equity= e.g. $400,000/$325,000=1.23

2.5.7.2 Intelligence: **The level of indebt ness is not absolute**. The "normal" debt-to-equity ratio is somewhere about 1:0.The above example shows 1:23 and would indicate a company with slightly more leverage than a banker might feel comfortable with.

As an Analyst, one should ask questions. What is the standard industry level of debt?

2.5.8 Data-Profitability ratios : Profitability ratios offer several different measures of the success of the firm at generating profits. The gross profit margin is a measure of the gross profit earned on sales. The gross profit margin considers the firm's cost of goods sold, but does not include other costs.

2.5.8.1 Information: Profitability/ROI. The two basic measures here are ROE and ROA. These would become critical if your company were to acquire another firm or to begin its due diligence work for a joint venture or alliance. As a potential investor or acquirer, you need to know the relative return you can expect from your investment.

---

[50] Leonard m.fuld Pg 302

ROE[51] = Net Income / Total stockholders' equity = $200,000/$10,000 = 20%.

ROA. This ratio helps determine how much profit a company is able to generate from each dollar of assets on its balance sheet. The before-tax ROA ratio is calculated as follows:

ROA (before taxes) = Operating earnings before interest/taxes/Total assets = $350,000/$20,000 = 17.5 %.

2.5.8.2 Intelligence: ROE: A 20% return is considered a healthy return on equity for most companies. Always compare your findings with industry averages before you draw a conclusion about your target company's standings. Exceptional case is the biotechnology Industry.

Reasons : Based on the return-on-equity formula as discussed earlier, the biotechnology industry should not exist today. The biotechnology industry has spawned hundreds of start-up companies over the past decade. Many of them are still not profitable, yet they continue to receive funding through stockholders or venture capitalists.

Biotech is a great example of why intelligence analysis should understand and use ratios,

2.5.8.3 Calculating ROE for Bio technology Industries[52]: For some biotech companies, one would be investing in their future products and income, their future

---

[51] Leonard m. fuld Pg 302
[52] Leonard m.fuld Pg 303

ROE. One needs to understand the product portfolio and the income it may generate.

For example: If the FDA has just approved a new genetically engineered healthcare treatment in a much needed treatment area, the future ROE may be immense, even though, right now, it's in the basement.

2.5.9 Intelligence and assumptions in two perspectives

2.5.9.1 Banker perspective: one might feel the biotech company that it is currently a big risk and a loan is probably out of question.

2.5.9.2 Stockholder perspective: One would speculate in investing by buying shares or supplying funds as venture capital.

ROA. One way to make use of this ratio is to compare it to your own ROA; another use would be in an acquisition analysis, to compare it to members of an industry peer group. Let's take ROA analysis a step further. If the same company can earn 17.5 cents on each dollar of assets, it can earn 17.5 cents on assets supported by borrowed funds. If the borrowed funds only cost the company 8 % on average(taking into account zero-interest trade payables, equipment loans, lines of credit, mortgages, and so on),then it has the ability to generate healthy 9.5 % returns on leveraged assets. In other words, the amount the company earns on borrowed funds is greater than the amount it pays in interest expense. This is called financial leverage, and it is very important to prospective investors, acquirers, or shareholders in a company. One should bear in mind that extraordinary gains or losses, heavily depreciated fixed assets, or a high level of intangible assets (e.g., goodwill) can distort the ROA figure one should always remember to analyse the ratio in the proper context, taking into account the company's unique business dynamics and those of the industry in general

Taking the above concept in view Intelligence should answer the questions

2.5.9.3 What is the current ROE[53]? What might it be five years from now, when the approved drugs or treatment have been fully tested and placed on the market?(Projected cash flow is the key at this stage.)

2.5.9.4 How deep should this start—up's pockets be? What additional money will it need to pump into R & D, testing, and ultimately, marketing and selling? Will it become a money pit?

2.5.9.5 who manages the company? How successful have the managers been with past start-ups?

- Are the patents and treatments technically unique? Are they likely to maintain a market edge, or will thy be superseded by a more potent medication or treatment

---

[53] Leonard m.fuld pg 303

2.5.9.6 Modifying the ratios through Interviews[54]

No ratio will be the perfect equation of a target company's balance sheet or income statement. One need to adjust the numbers one arrives at. Interviewing the experts will tell you whether your numbers are out of line or on the money. Interviewing is an excellent means of adjusting the inventory numbers one may have derived (although, in the same industry, one company's inventory may be totally different from its competitors')

2.5.9.7 Example of steps in uncovering Financial Data using Ratios[55]

	Step 1	Step 2	Step 3	Step 4
	Known data	Industry ratios	financial data Derived through Ratios	Final result Data adjusted based on Interviews
Current Assets	$100,000			$100,000
Current ratio		2:1		5:3
			$50,000	$60,000
	—			

2.6. Competitor Response Profile: Information from an analysis of the competitor's objectives, assumptions, strategy, and capabilities can be compiled into a response profile of

---

[54] Leonard m.fuld Pg 305
[55] Leonard m.fuld Pg 306

possible moves that might be made by the competitor. This profile includes Both offensive and defensive moves

2.6.1. Offensive moves[56]
The first step is to predict the strategic change the competitor might initiate.

2.6.1.1 Satisfaction with current position : Comparing the competitor's goals with its current position, is the competitor likely to attempt to initiate strategic change?

2.6.1.2 Probable moves. Based on the competitior's goals, assumption, and capabilities relative to its existing position. What are the most probable strategic changes the competitor will make? These will reflect the competitor's view about the future, what it believes its strength to be, which of its rivals it thinks are vulnerable, how it likes to compete, The biases brought to the business by top management, and other considerations suggested by the preceding analysis.

2.6.1.3 Strength & seriousness of moves: The analysis of a competitor's goals and capabilities can be used to assess the expected strength of these probable moves. It is also important to assess what the competitor may gain from the move.

2.6.2 Defensive Capability[57]
The next step in building a response profile is to construct a list of the range of feasible strategic moves a firm in the

---

[56] Porter 1980 Pg 67
[57] Porter 1980 Pg 68

industry might make and a list of the possible industry and environmental changes that might occur. These can be assessed against the following criteria to determine the competitor's defensive capability, with inputs coming from the analysis in the previous section

2.6.2.1 Vulnerability: To what strategic moves and governmental macroeconomic or industry events would the competitor be most vulnerable? What events have asymmetrical profit consequences that is. Affect a competitor's profits more or less than they affect the initiating firm's what moves would require so much capital to retaliate against or follow that the competitor cannot risk them?

2.6.2.2 Provocation What moves or events are such that they will provoke a retaliation from competitors even though retaliation may be costly and lead to marginal financial performance? That is, what moves threaten a competitor's goals or position so much that it will be forces to retaliate? Like it or not? Most competitors will have hot buttons, or areas of the business where a threat will lead to disproportionate response. Hot buttons reflects strong held goals, emotional commitments, and the like. Where possible, they are to be avoided.

2.6.2.3 Effectiveness of retaliation: To what moves or events in the competitor impeded from reacting to quickly and /or effectively given its goals, strategy, existing capabilities, and assumptions?

2.7. Competitor Analysis and Industry Forecasting[58].

An analysis of each significant existing and potential competitor can be used as an important input to forecast future industry conditions. The knowledge of each competitor's probable moves and capability to respond to change can be summer up, and competitor's can be seen as interacting with each other on a simulated basis to answer the following:

- What are the implications of the interactions of the probable competitor's moves that have been identified?
- Are firms' strategic converging and likely to clash?
- Do firms' have sustainable growth rates that match the Industry's forecasted growth rate, or will a gap be created that will invite entry?
- Will probable moves combine to hold implications for Industry structure?

---

[58] Porter 1980 Pg 71

Reference Books

1. Buzzell, Robert D, and Bradley T.Gale 1987 PIMS principle, New York. Free press
2. Bolman, L.G and T.Deal, 1997. Reframing Organisations Artistry, choice, and leadership, 2nd edition, San Franscisco, CA Jossey-Das Publishers
3. Camp, R. 1989, Benchmarking: the search for industry best practices that lead to superior performance. Quality press. Milwaukee, Wisconsin
4. Craig S. Fleischer & Barbette E. Bensoussen. Strategy and Competitor analysis
5. FINKELSTEIN, S. & HAMBRICK, D.1996. Strategic leadership: top executives and their effects on organisations. West Publishing Company Minneapolis
6. Grinyer, P.H & Norburn, D 1977/1978. "Planning for existing markets. An empirical study". International studies in Management and Organisation Vol 17 pp.99-122
7. Hall, William K.1980, 2 Survival strategies in a hostile environment,
   "Harvard Business Review" (September-October), Pg 75-85
8. Larry Kahader How to gather, Analyse, and use information to move your business to the top edition 1997
9. Mintzberg, Henry, B.Ahlstrand, and J.Lampel. 1998 Strategy safari: A Guided tour through the wilds of strategic Management. New York, NY The free press

10. Porter M.E., 1985 Competitive advantage: creating and sustaining performance
11. Porter M.E., 1985 Competitive advantage: creating and sustaining performance
12. Porter M.E. Competitive advantage, New York Press. 1980
13. Porter M.E 1979.The structure within Industries and companies performance. Review of economics and statistics May. 214-227
14. Sanchez & Heene, A, 1996.A sytems theory of the firm in competence-based competition.In Sanchez:Heene & Thomas,1996,Pg 39-62
15. Snuif, H.R, and P.S Zwart(1994 a) Strategische besluitvorming in net MKB: Een process model,MAB,mci Pp 264-274
16. The new Competitive Intelligence, the complete resource for finding and analysing... by Leonard M.Fuld, Fuld & Company, Cambridge, MA
17. Thompson J.D, 1967, Organisations in action New York. McGraw Hill
18. Volberda, H.W, and T.Elfring, 2001.Rethinking strategy, London, sage publications
19. Porter M.E., 1985 Competitive advantage: creating and sustaining performance
20. Porter M.E. Competitive advantage, New York Press. 1980
21. Porter M.E 1979.The structure within Industries and companies performance. Review of economics and statistics May. 214-227
22. The new Competitive Intelligence, the complete resource for finding and analysing... by Leonard M.Fuld, Fuld & Company, Cambridge, MA

23. Thompson J.D, 1967, Organisations in action New York. McGraw Hill
24. Volberda, H.W, and T.Elfring, 2001.Rethinking strategy, London, sage publications

Journals

1. Ashton, B., & Sen R.K., 1988.Using Patent information in technology and business planning I. "Research Technology Management", 31 (69) Pg 42-46
2. Beal, R.M (2000), Competing efficiently: environmental scanning competitive strategy and organisational Performance in small Manufacturing firm, Journal of small Business Mangement, Vol 38 (1), Pp27-47
3. Bradley, Robert D., and Bradley T. Gale and Ralph G.M. Sultan, 1975 "Market share-A key to Profitability", HBR, 53(January/February), Pg 97-106.
4. Brandenburger, Adam M, and Barry J.Nelebuff. 1995. The Right game: use Game theory to shape strategy. Harvard business Review July-August: 57-71
5. Gilinsky. E Stanny, R.L McLine and R.Eyler (2001). Does firm size matter? An empirical investigation into the competitive strategies of the small firm.Journal of Small Business Strategy, Vol 12 (20 Pp 1-11
6. Gray, J.H(1997), small business strategy in Australia,Academy of Entrepreneurship Journal,Vol 2(2).Pp 44-58

7. Haley, R., 1968. Benefit Segmentation: A decision oriented research tool. Journal of Marketing July, Vol 32, pp 30-35
8. Hamel & Prahlad, 1991 corporate imagination and expeditionary Marketing
9. Hitt, M.A., R.D.Ireland, S.M.Camp and D.L. Sexton, 2001 Strategic entrepreneurship: Entrepreneurial strategies for wealth creation. Strategic Management Journal 22 (Special issue). Pg 479.491
10. Hoouthoofd, N, & Heene, A 1997: Strategic groups as subsets of strategic scope groups in the Belgian brewing Industry Strategic Management studies July Pg 429-451
11. HAMBRICK, D.C., 1982. Environmental scanning and organisational Strategy Strategic Management Journal Vol 3 Pg 159-174
12. Lawrence C.Rhyne, Mary B.Teagarten, William Van den Panhuyzen. Journal of High technology Management Research.Dept of Management, College of Business Administration.San Diego State University,San Diego, A 92182
13. KEFLAS, A & SCHOLERBEK, P.P., 1973. Scanning the business environment some empirical results, Decision Sciences Vol. 4, Pg 63-74
14. Karki, M.M.S., 1997. "Patent Citation analysis. A policy analysis tool. "World Patent information, 19(4), Pg 269-272
15. Montgomery, C.A., and M.E.Porter(eds):1991 Strategy:seeking and securing competitive advantage : Boston,MA:Harvard Business School press.

16. MIntzberg, H (1994) Strategie vorming:tien scholen,Script im Management
17. Miller, D., & Friesen, P., 1977. "Strategy making in context: Ten empirical archetypes, "Journal of Management studies, 14839, 253-280
18. Murphy,G.B,J.W.Trailer and R.C Hill(1996),Measuring performance in entrepreneurship research,Journal of Business Research,Vol 36,Pp 15-23
    Nelson, R.R., 1991. Why do firms differ, and how does it matter? Strategic Management Journal, 12-Pg 61-748 Winter Special Issue
19. Parker,A.R(2000) Impact on the organisational performance of the strategy technology policy interaction,Journal of Business research,Vol.47 Pp 55-64.
20. Pelham,A.M(2000),Market orientation and other potential influences on Performance in small and medium-sized manufacturing firms,Journal of small business Management,Vol 38(1),Pp 48-67.
21. Porter M.E (1991),Towards a dynamic theory of strategy,Strategic Management Journal, Vol 12.Pp 95-117.
22. Postma, T.J.B.M. and D.S. Zwart, 2001, Strategic research and performance of SMEs Journal of small business strategy, Vol. 1292 Pg 52-64
23. Sanchez, R:Heene, A, & Thomas H (1996). Dynamics of Competence-based competition: Theory and practice in the nem strategic Management
24. Sanchez & Heene,A(1997) Reinventing strategic management:new theory and practice for

competence-based competition. European Management Journal, Vol 15, No 3. PP. 303-317

25. Snuif, H.R, and P.S Zwart(1994 a) Strategische Besluitvorming in net MKB: Een process model,MAB,mci Pp 264-274
20. issue)
26. SIMON, H.A., 1967. "Motivational and emotional controls of cognition", Psychological Review, 74, Pg 29-39
27. Wieranga, B., 1983. Model and measurement methodology for the analysis of consumer choice for food products, Journal of food quality no.6, Pg 119-137

Working paper

1. Arnold Wetzel Lecturer in Economics, MU & RAU. Link between Macro Vs Micro Economics Source. Realistic Strategies from Unrealistic Micro economic theories. Pg 17
2. Campbell, R.S., 1983. "Patenting the future: A new way to forecast changing technology. "The futurist, 12(6) Pg 62-67
3. The Power of Trade shows: Fact sheet 3 Trade show bureau, Copyright 1992
4. Marylyn Placet and Kristi.M.Branch Chapter 3 version 2.doc,06.08.02
5. Willyard, C.H., and C.W. McClees, 1987. Motorola Technology Roadmap process research Management Sept/Oct, Pg 13-19
7. Research Report: Strategy and small performance P.Gibcus, R.G.M. Kemp. Zoetermeer, January 2003

Internet sources.

1. www.Encyclopedia.lockergnome.com/s/b/experience_curve_effects
2. www.exinfm.com
3. www.market-intelligence.co.uk
4. www.tns-infratest.com/pmwa
5. www.netmba.com
6. www.quickmba.com
7. Industry analysis—CSA5eCO3 (1).PDF
8. 9. WP data/IPCWEB/MSWORD/WP-9MS.Doc., March 1994
10. J.D. Waldman Strategic Management Anderson 598 Summer 2001 Pg 20
11. Houthoofd and Heene, A systems view on what matters to excel. May 2000, Pg 22.
12. AICC Purdue University Purdue University Agricultural Innovation and Commercialisation Center, Industry Analysis; the five forces, 2002
13. www.sbaer.uca.edu/research/2000/swma/Doswma63.htm 2002, Pg 1-11

Please note that I am attaching a research paper from pages 23 to 29. I have used the citation words, but I am unable to get the remaining part or the name of the research paper.

The following authors have to be noted because of the Date and Page constraints

1. Mac Millan 1982,
2. Porter, 1985,
3. Hitt, M-A, R.D.Ireland, S.M. Camp and D.L. Sexton, 2001
4. Grant 1988
5. Miller & Friesen, 1977

www.ingramcontent.com/pod-product-compliance
Lightning Source LLC
Chambersburg PA
CBHW021014180526
45163CB00005B/1954